G

J 5156109G
595.799 O'Toole, Christopher.
OTO The honeybee in the meadow

Y0-CVG-511

M

SEQUOYAH REGIONAL LIBRARY
3 8749 0051 5610 9

Animal Habitats

The Honeybee in the Meadow

Text by Christopher O'Toole

Photographs by Oxford Scientific Films

Belitha Press

Contents

Meadow bees	2	Drones and mating	20
Bees and flowers	4	New queens and the colony cycle	22
The honeybee's body	8	Enemies	24
Growing up as a worker	10		
The importance of the queen	12	Friends and neighbours in the meadow	26
Working in the nest	14	Honeybees and people	28
Out in the meadow	16	Life in the meadow	30
Dancing in the dark	18	Glossary	32

Note: The use of a capital letter for a bee's name indicates that it is a *species* of bee (e.g. Western Honeybee) and the use of lower case means that it is a member of a larger *group* of bees.

This flower-rich meadow in the Rocky Mountains of Colorado, is ideal for honeybees.

A worker honeybee collects pollen from a crocus.

Meadow bees

Have you ever sat listening to the hum of insects in a meadow on a hot, lazy afternoon? This summery sound comes from a variety of insects: brightly-coloured hoverflies flit from flower to flower and bumblebees bumble and drone their way from blossom to blossom. But if there is a nearby beekeeper, then much of the humming noise will be coming from worker honeybees as they make their way across the meadow, collecting pollen and *nectar* from the flowers.

There are at least 20,000 different species of bee in the world and five of these are honeybees. Bees are really special hunting wasps which have become vegetarians. Instead of catching other insects as food for their offspring, they gather pollen and nectar. Pollen is rich in body-building proteins, while the sweet nectar is a liquid, energy-rich mixture of sugars. Honeybees can 'ripen' this sugar-rich mixture and turn it into honey.

A tremendous amount of work goes into making honey: it takes about 38,000 foraging trips to gather enough nectar to make just one pound of honey (82,000 trips for one kilogram); the bees from a single hive may visit 4,800,000 flowers in one day's work. This is why the meadow is alive with honeybees on a warm summer's day.

The Western Honeybee is found in many parts of the world. It lives in Europe, Western Asia and the whole of Africa. This is the species kept by beekeepers. Settlers from Europe introduced it into North America in the 1620s, but the honeybee was not taken to Australia and New Zealand until the last century. The Indians of North America soon took to beekeeping and used to call the honeybee 'the white man's fly'.

In the wild, the Western Honeybee nests in hollow tree trunks, caves and sheltered clefts in rock faces. Here, it builds vertical, double-sided *honeycombs* out of wax. Each comb consists of hundreds of six-sided chambers or cells. The bees store food and rear their broods in these cells.

Already dusted with pollen, this worker honeybee probes an Ox-eye Daisy for nectar.

Bees and flowers

Bees visit flowers because they depend entirely on pollen and nectar for food. At the same time, most kinds of flower depend on bees for fertilization: as the bees move from flower to flower, they accidentally carry pollen from the male parts (anthers) of one flower to the female part (stigma) of another flower of the same kind. This is called 'pollination' and enables seeds to grow.

Flowers make themselves attractive to bees by producing scents and by advertizing their presence with brightly-coloured petals. It is fortunate for us that bees and people like the same scents. Imagine how unpleasant life would be if bees were attracted to flowers which smelt nasty! The sweet nectar produced by many flowers is a reward for the bees which pollinate them.

If you look closely at any kind of bee, you will see that its body is covered with hairs. Under a microscope, you can see that the hairs are branched and feathery. This means that when a bee visits a flower to collect nectar, it brushes past the anthers and thousands of pollen grains become trapped between the hairs.

A worker honeybee seeks nectar at a Meadow Cranebill. The dark lines on the petals are called 'nectar guides' and the bee follows these to the nectaries at the base of the petals.

A worker honeybee gathers pollen and nectar from a sallow catkin. Sallows are a very important source of food for bees in early spring.

Worker honeybees have an ingenious way of carrying the pollen back to the nest. On the outer surface of part of their hindlegs, there is a pollen basket. This is a smooth, slightly hollowed-out area, fringed by long, stiff bristles. If a worker is collecting pollen, she hovers briefly after leaving a flower while she uses her front and middle pairs of legs to brush pollen from her body hairs, especially the hairs on the *thorax*. She passes the pollen back to her hind legs, where she packs it into the pollen baskets, moistened slightly with nectar. When both baskets are full, she returns to the nest.

A worker bee may have to visit several hundred flowers on a single trip to gather enough pollen to fill the baskets. Usually, on any one foraging trip, a worker tends to visit only one type of flower. This increases the chances that the flowers will be pollinated.

As well as pollen and nectar, bees collect a sticky resin called 'propolis'. This is produced by certain buds and plant wounds. The bees carry it back to the nest in their pollen baskets; they use it as a building material to make the nest entrance smaller or, to fill up cracks in the hives.

Worker honeybees may visit several hundred flowers before their pollen baskets are full.

A queen honeybee. She has no pollen baskets, but her abdomen is swollen with eggs.

The honeybee's body

Like bumblebees, the honeybee is a social insect and lives in colonies. Each colony is a family group and consists of a single, egg-laying female or *queen*, many thousands of workers and, for part of the summer, a number of males or *drones* (a few hundred to 2,000). These three kinds of members, called *castes*, each have their own special tasks to perform. The queen's main job is to lay eggs, while the drone's only duty is to mate with a queen. The workers, however, are sterile females and have many different tasks. Because of their different roles, it is not surprising that the bodies of the different castes differ from one another slightly. Nevertheless, being insects, their bodies share the same basic plan.

Like all insects, the honeybee's body is enclosed in an outer shell or *exoskeleton*. This is made of a horny substance called 'chitin', which is light in weight, very tough and waterproof. The body is divided into three main parts, the head, thorax and *abdomen*.

Using her tongue, this worker honeybee probes a flower for nectar.

The head contains the brain and carries a pair of large *compound eyes*. Each eye is made up of thousands of facets and every facet has its own lens. Eyes of this type are very good at detecting movement. The eyes of a queen honeybee have about 3,000-4,000 facets; she does not need very good eyesight because most of her life is spent in the darkness of the nest. Worker bees spend much of their time out in the field so they need to see well; their eyes have 4,000-6,900 facets. Drones need to see well, too, in order to find queens in flight – they have the largest eyes, with 7,000-8,600 facets.

On top of a honeybee's head are three simple eyes or *ocelli*, which can sense changes in the amount of light. Between the eyes are a pair of feelers or *antennae*, which are used for feeling and smelling. Smell is very important in the lives of honeybees – they communicate with each other by means of special messenger scents called *pheromones*.

The antennae of the queen and workers are made up of twelve sections or segments, while the drone's antennae have thirteen. A drone's antennae are about 300 times more sensitive to smell than those of the workers. His antennae, like his large eyes, are mainly used for finding a mate.

A honeybee's head also carries a pair of jaws and a set of tubular sucking mouthparts called the tongue or *proboscis*. Queens and drones never feed at flowers and have short tongues, but worker bees have longer tongues, from 0.20-0.28 in (5.3-7.2 mm) which can probe into flowers for nectar. Parts of the tongue are sensitive to taste.

A worker honeybee with full pollen baskets.

A drone or male honeybee on a honeycomb. You can see his extra large eyes.

The middle-part of the body, or thorax, bears the two pairs of wings and three pairs of legs along with the muscles which work them. The transparent wings are strengthened by dark veins. When a honeybee flies, the forewings are coupled to the hind wings by means of a row of little hooks on the front edge of the hind wings. The wings of a worker can beat about 200 times per second.

Each of the six legs has a pair of hooked claws at its tip. The front pair of legs have a special device for cleaning the antennae. This consists of a semi-circular notch and a little spur. To clean its antenna, the bee draws it through the notch and the spur rubs against it like a brush. The legs of workers are specially designed for gathering pollen and carrying it back to the nest. Because they never gather food, the legs of both queen and drones are not specialized in this way.

The rear part of the body, or abdomen, is divided into segments – six in the queen and workers and seven in the drones. The abdomen contains the honey stomach and the gut. The abdomen of the drone also contains the male sex organs. The queen and workers, both being female, have a pair of ovaries inside their abdomens. The queen's ovaries are extremely large and well-developed; each contains 150-180 egg-making tubes called 'ovarioles'. Normally, the ovaries of workers are small and under-developed – they rarely produce eggs and have only 2-12 ovarioles each. The abdomen of a worker bee also contains a special scent *gland*, the Nasonov gland, and four pairs of wax glands.

Both the queen and the workers have a sting in the tip of the abdomen. The sting has a poison gland and is armed with sharp hooks or barbs along its length. A worker bee uses her sting to inject some poison into an enemy when she is attacked or is defending the nest. The queen's sting has only very tiny barbs; she uses her sting not to defend the colony, but to kill other, rival young queens. Drones have no stings.

A close-up view of the right front and hind wings of a worker honeybee. The veins make the wing rigid. You can see the row of little hooks on the front edge of the hindwing which join the wings together.

A worker honeybee has stung this person in the finger and left the sting behind to carry on pumping venom.

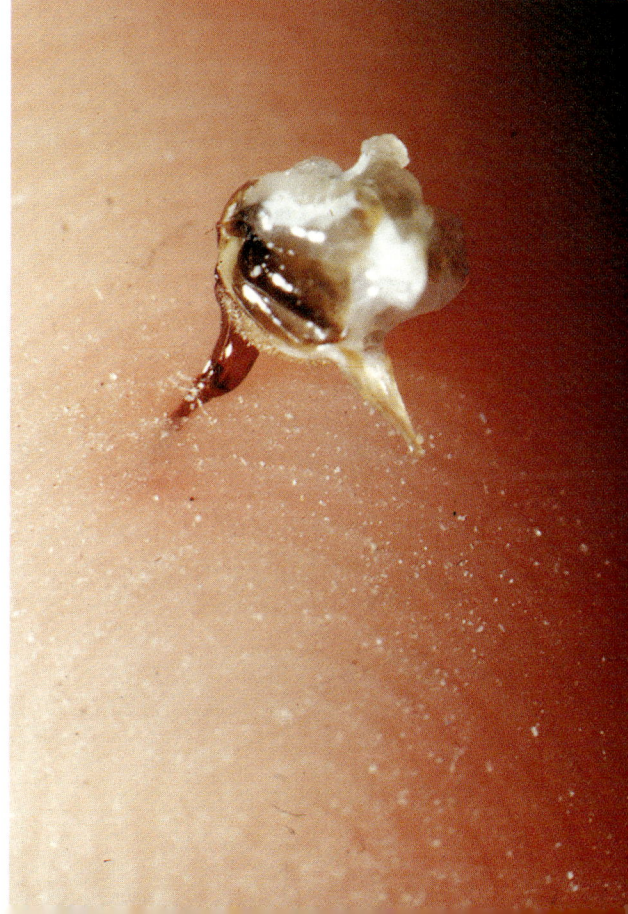

The egg of a honeybee is laid by the queen at the bottom of a brood cell.

Cells of brood comb containing full-grown larvae of worker honeybees.

Growing up as a worker

A honeybee, whether it is a worker, drone or queen, starts life as an egg. This is laid by the queen in the bottom of a cell in a part of the comb called the 'brood comb'. Only one bee at a time develops in a cell, but a cell may be used many times. Like many other insects, bees go through three stages in their development before becoming adult: egg, *larva* and *pupa*.

There may be up to 30,000 brood cells in a healthy colony and most of these contain developing workers. Drone cells are larger than worker cells and queens develop in an altogether different and special kind of cell.

The egg hatches after three days and the larva spends all of its time eating. For the first three days, the larva is fed almost entirely on a special kind of rich food called *royal jelly*, together with small amounts of pollen and honey. Royal jelly, sometimes called 'bee milk', is made in glands in the heads of worker bees. Larvae which are to become workers or drones receive royal jelly for their first three days. Afterwards, the amount of royal jelly is greatly reduced and the diet then consists almost entirely of pollen and honey provided by workers. Larvae destined to be queens, however, are fed on royal jelly for the whole of their larval life.

The larva is a blind, legless grub, with a pair of simple jaws. It is really nothing more than an eating machine. It grows rapidly and moults its skin six times before becoming a pupa. In Europe, the larval stage of workers lasts about five and a half days, but in hot countries, it is shorter. Nurse bees then cap the cell with wax, the enclosed larva spins a cocoon of silk and the larva is ready to pupate.

The pupa is equivalent to the chrysalis of moths and butterflies. During this stage, an amazing change takes place: much of the larval body is

The caps of some of these brood cells have been removed to show the pupae of worker honeybees. You can also see a new worker which is about to emerge, breaking open its cell cap.

broken down and rearranged to form an adult honeybee. At first, the pupa is pearly white and looks like a mummified adult, but soon the eyes become black and the rest of the body darkens. After eight to nine days, the pupal skin splits to reveal a fully-formed honeybee. The young bee remains in the cell for several hours while its skin hardens.

When it is ready to emerge, a young worker bites its way through the wax cap of the cell. Other workers may remove the tattered cap remains and use the wax to build more cells or make more caps – very little is wasted in the honeybee colony. Once out of the comb, the young bee spreads its antennae and wings. Soon, her body hairs are dry and now she is ready for a life of toil.

Looking rather bedraggled, a new worker honeybee emerges, helped by an older worker.

11

Marked with a spot of yellow paint to make her stand out, the queen lays eggs, attended by her court of workers.

The importance of the queen

The queen spends much of her time moving over the comb and laying eggs. Whenever she stops, any nearby workers gather around her to form a 'court'. They constantly touch her with their antennae, offer her food and lick her with their tongues. The licking keeps her clean but the touching with antennae is the most important activity. The queen has glands in her head and these produce a mixture of special chemicals called *queen substance,* which becomes spread over her body.

  The workers which form her court pick up this scent (or pheromone) with their antennae and tongues. Because workers are always touching one another with their antennae and exchanging food from mouth to mouth, the queen substance spreads rapidly throughout the colony. It has very important effects on the workers: it prevents their ovaries from developing and stops them from building queen cells and rearing new young queens. It also encourages workers to go out and search for food. In this way, the queen has a sort of chemical power which controls the lives and behaviour of the workers.

  A healthy queen lives for up to five years. In a good year she will lay up to 200,000 eggs. In the late spring and summer months, when the meadow is rich in flowers and provides plenty of food, the queen may lay as many as 1,500 eggs each day. Most of these eggs develop into workers, but sometimes, drones or new queens are produced.

Sooner or later, an ageing queen begins to lay fewer eggs and to produce less queen substance. A strong colony may have 40-80,000 workers and if there is less queen substance to be passed among them, the queen's chemical control over the workers becomes weaker and weaker. The same thing happens if there is a rapid growth in the number of workers. Either way, the result is the same – the workers start to build queen cells.

A queen cell is conical in shape, about 1 in (25 mm) long, and hangs down from the normal comb. The workers usually build a queen cell over a brood cell already containing a fertilized egg or a very young larva no older than three days. They feed the larva only on royal jelly. The larva turns into a pupa and then after about 16 days, a new queen emerges. The workers may rear up to ten queens at a time.

If the old queen should die, then the loss of queen substance in the colony is very rapid. The workers become agitated and aggressive. Large numbers of workers begin fanning with their wings and this causes a loud 'roaring' noise which is dreaded by beekeepers because it means that all is not well.

Between 12 and 48 hours after loss of the queen, the workers begin to build as many as 20 queen cells. However, if the colony has no eggs or young larvae ready to grow into queens, then the ovaries of many workers enlarge and some workers start to lay eggs. Because workers never mate, they lay only unfertilized eggs, which eventually become drones. Such colonies soon die out because there is no queen. But at least some of the drones which develop from worker eggs may fly off and mate with queens from other colonies.

Two workers exchange food, tongue to tongue. This is one way in which queen substance is passed through the colony.

A worker honeybee eats pollen stored in a cell.

Working in the nest

The jobs that a worker honeybee does at any one time depend on its age. So, during the course of its life, it passes through several 'professions'. As a rule, young workers stay at home and in the nest, while older ones have tasks outside.

For the first nine days or so, a young worker cleans out cells so that they can be used again. During this time, she also fits wax caps to cells filled with honey or fully grown larvae. Some of this wax she produces herself; but at this age her wax glands are small and much of the wax she uses is placed on the rims of the cells by older workers.

While she is a cleaner, special glands in the worker's head start to become active and soon she is ready to produce royal jelly, which she feeds to young larvae. During this time a young worker bee feeds often on pollen and, especially, honey. She needs a lot of food to build up her wax glands. Sometimes, workers seem to take time off from looking after the nest; in fact, they are making wax. The wax comes out of their glands in white sheets. The worker removes them with her hind legs and passes them to her front legs and jaws. She chews the wax and moulds it into the comb. She has now become a builder.

A worker (centre) has returned to the hive with a load of pollen.

Around this time, the worker bee concentrates on feeding the queen larvae – she also starts receiving nectar from workers who have been out foraging. After she has taken nectar from these other workers, she finds a quiet part of the nest. Here she sits and repeatedly opens and closes her mouthparts, exposing the nectar to the air. This allows water to evaporate from the nectar. The nectar gradually becomes thicker and much more sugary. In this way, nectar is 'ripened' into honey. After about 20 minutes, the worker places the nectar into a cell. The ripening continues for several more days. Other bees help the evaporation process by fanning their wings to produce a stream of drying air over the honeycomb. Worker bees may carry out fanning duties at almost any age. Soon, the worker also handles pollen brought back by foragers. The forager places her load in a cell and the young worker packs it down, mixing it with a little honey and saliva.

For her last few days as a hive bee, the worker may return to working as a cleaner. But now, she is ready for outside duties.

Worker honeybees inspect honeycomb with both open and capped cells containing honey.

Worker bees fanning to ventilate the nest.

Out in the meadow

During her early life, a worker bee will already have prepared for work outside the nest. She will have ventured outside the hive several times to make short orientation flights. These enable her to memorize both local and distant landmarks, so that later on, she can find her way back to the nest.

In hot weather, one of her first outside activities is to ventilate the nest. She and many other workers will stand just out the hive entrance, with their backs to it, fanning their wings rapidly. This directs a stream of fresh air into the nest and cools it down. In very hot weather, the workers place droplets of water in many cells – as the water evaporates, this also has a cooling effect. With hundreds of worker bees fanning, they can keep their colony at the correct temperature of about 95°F (about 35°C), even when the outside air temperature is up to 158°F (70°C), in extreme desert conditions.

Guard duty is one of the last tasks before a worker finally concentrates on foraging for pollen and nectar. Guards are easily spotted: they stand alert at the nest entrance with their jaws open, front legs raised and their antennae held forward. They also patrol small areas at the entrance to the hive and inspect incoming bees with their antennae. The guards recognize their nestmates by the colony smell on their bodies. They also recognize – and will attack – workers from other colonies or other insect intruders, which may try to enter the nest in order to steal honey.

A hardworking honeybee rests before continuing its foraging trip.

When a worker bee attacks and stings an enemy, she gives off an alarm pheromone from a gland near her sting. This attracts other guards and even workers which were not on guard duty – they also sting the enemy and raise even more help. The defending guards may also bite the enemy with their jaws, while giving off another alarm pheromone from glands in the head. If the enemy is as large as a bird or a mouse, the barbs on the worker's sting catch in the flesh. This means that the sting, with its poison and scent glands, is ripped out of the bee's body when it struggles free. The bee soon dies, but the poison sac continues to pump venom into the wound and the scent glands continue to emit alarm pheromone. Alarm pheromones evaporate very quickly, however, and the colony soon calms down when danger has passed.

A worker may spend only a few hours or at most a few days as a guard and some workers never become guards at all. For the rest of their short lives they will be foragers, going out into the hedgerows and meadows to search for food. In the summer months, workers live only for about five weeks.

Guard bees on duty at the hive entrance.

A worker tells some of her sisters of a source of nectar near the nest by performing the round dance.

Dancing in the dark

When a foraging worker has made several successful trips to the same, rich source of pollen and nectar, she is able to tell other bees of her good fortune. She does this by performing a special dance back in the nest, on the surface of the honeycomb.

If the good patch of flowers is 82 ft (25 m) or less from the hive, she indicates the distance by performing the round dance. She runs in a series of circles, either clockwise or anti-clockwise, changing direction every one or two circles. This attracts the attention of other nearby workers, who may try to follow her actions. Every now and then, the dancer stops and regurgitates a drop of nectar, which the other bees lap up eagerly. These other workers learn the scent of the flowers where she has foraged from the nectar; they can also smell it on the dancer's body with their antennae.

Some of the workers now leave the nest. They search within a radius of 82 ft (25 m) for flowers with the right scent. Usually, they find the flowers quickly and they, too, begin to gather nectar and pollen.

However, if the food source is much further away, then simply searching for the scent would take a very long time. For greater distances, therefore, it is useful if a successful forager can tell her nestmates the direction of the food source as well as its distance. She does this by performing the waggle dance.

In this dance, the worker runs in a squashed figure-of-eight, so that the run between the two halves of the 'eight' is straight. She does this over and over again for several minutes. Every time she makes the straight run, she waggles her abdomen rapidly. The length of time spent in the straight run, and the number of waggles, is greater the further away the food source is from the nest.

The direction of the food source is given by the straight run in a very clever way: the difference between the angle of the straight run and a vertical line is the same as the angle between the food source, the nest entrance and the sun. Scientists also think that the louder the buzzing sound given off by a waggle-dancer, the better may be the quality of the food.

During the waggle dance, other workers follow the dancer's movements very carefully. Somehow, by ways we do not yet understand, the workers can translate this 'dancing-in-the-dark' into information about distance and direction. Then they quickly find the original rich source of food.

In the round dance, the angle between the straight run and vertical is the same as the angle between the sun and the flowers, as seen from the hive entrance.

A drone honeybee feeds for several days before going on a mating flight.

Drones and mating

In a good season, when the meadow flowers provide honeybees with plenty of food, the colony rears drones. In the early spring, the workers will have built larger, drone cells. The cells need to be larger because drones are bigger than workers and need more space in which to grow. When the queen lays an egg in one, she can tell it is a drone cell by measuring it with her forelegs and she 'knows' also that she must lay an egg which will develop into a drone.

She can do this because drones develop from unfertilized eggs. When the queen lays an egg – just before it comes out – it passes a little chamber called the *spermatheca*. Here, the queen stores sperm after mating. If the egg is to be a drone, then no sperm is released to fertilize it as it passes by; if the egg is to be a female, for rearing as a worker or queen, then the queen releases a small amount of sperm and the egg is fertilized.

Because drones are bigger than workers, their larvae need more food than worker larvae. Later, when the young drones first emerge, they beg the workers for food and are given a mixture of royal jelly, pollen and honey for the first few days. After about a week, they fend for themselves and feed on stored honey. Drones feed for about 12 days until they have made enough sperm and are ready to go out on mating flights.

Like young worker bees, drones make several orientation flights outside the nest. Then they fly off to mate. Many hundreds or even thousands of drones from several colonies may gather in the same place over the meadow. They fly at 109-130 ft (10-40 m) above the ground. When a virgin queen flies through or near the mass of drones, they quickly detect her both by sight and smell. They follow her in a thick cluster or 'comet'. One drone pounces on her from below and mates with her in the air. As they mate, the drone's sperm passes quickly into the queen's body. Immediately after mating, the drone falls backwards and drops to the ground, leaving his penis behind in the queen. He soon dies, having performed the one task of his life. The vast majority of drones, however, never mate at all. At the end of the mating season, any drones remaining in the nest are dragged out of the colony by workers and killed.

A swarm of honeybees takes to the air in an orchard.

A queen cell, built out from the brood comb, is inspected by a worker.

Young queens and the colony cycle

Before a young queen is two weeks old, she flies out of the hive and mates; she usually makes several mating flights and mates with several different drones. When she finally returns to the nest, her spermatheca will contain nearly six million sperm, enough to fertilize her eggs for the rest of her life. Being the first to emerge, this young queen will kill any other young queens in their cells before leaving on her first mating flight. There is only room for one reigning queen in a honeybee colony!

Very soon, the young queen starts laying eggs. And, because she produces more queen substance than the old queen, the workers stop rearing new queens. Meanwhile, if the old queen has not already been killed by the workers, the new queen finds and kills her.

But, sometimes in early summer, the colony produces a swarm a few days before the first young queen emerges. A swarm consists of the old queen and about half (up to 30,000) of the workers and drones. The swarm leaves the nest and settles as a group on a nearby branch or fence.

A swarm is about to leave this hive.

The swarm has clustered in a fruit tree while scouts seek out a new nesting place.

After a while, special scout bees go off and look for a suitable new nesting place. When a scout finds a good place, she returns to the swarm and performs a dance similar to the round and waggle dances used for finding food. In this way, she alerts more scouts. Gradually, more of the workers discover the distance and direction of the new nesting place. The original scouts return time and again to the spot and mark it with a special scent from their Nasonov glands. This attracts other scouts.

When the swarm finally moves to the new nesting place, scouts guide it by giving out Nasonov scent. This, and the queen substance, keeps the swarm together as a group. While they are in the swarm and without a home, the bees have to live on honey stored in their crops.

At the new nest, workers rapidly build the comb and forage for pollen and nectar. They feed the queen and she starts egg-laying again. The colony soon settles down to its normal routine.

Swarming often happens when a colony becomes overcrowded or when there is not enough food. It is a way of splitting the colony into two and starting a new population of bees with a new queen in charge. Meanwhile, in the original nest, the new young queen will have taken over the colony.

During the summer, the colony builds up its store of pollen and honey. This will be a vital food supply for the coming winter. When it is too cold to fly, the entire colony clusters together for warmth at the centre of the nest. In northern countries, honeybees can survive when the outside temperature is as low as 14.4°F (-40°C.) The bees keep warm by eating their store of honey and by generating their own heat. They manage to survive until workers venture out again in the first mild days of the following spring.

A colony of Carmine Bee-eaters nesting in a river bank in West Africa. These birds kill thousands of bees, especially honeybees.

Enemies

With such large stores of sweet honey and thousands of fat grubs, it is not surprising that honeybees have many enemies. Even workers, armed as they are with a painful sting, are attacked and eaten by various animals. Birds such as shrikes and bee-eaters kill many bees in southern Europe and Africa.

In Europe and North America, woodpeckers are a threat to honeybees: they drill into wooden hives and eat the bees, especially in winter, when the bees are sleepy and inactive. Any bees which are not eaten usually die of cold, because of the many holes made by the birds.

The House Mouse and Wood Mouse are sometimes pests in beehives too. They even build their nests in hives without being stung. They eat pollen, honey and bees, and often destroy colonies. Wasps are another enemy at the honeybees nests; they lie in wait to pounce on returning workers and rip open their bulging honey crops. In Japan, 20-30 workers of the giant Mandarin Hornet can, between them, kill 5-25,000 honeybees in a few hours and then remove larvae, pupae and adult bees to their own nest, where they feed them to their own larvae.

Honeybees can themselves be enemies. Workers from one hive, especially if the colony is weak or the season is poor, may invade other, stronger hives and attempt to steal honey.

A Honey Badger in the Kalahari Desert of southern Africa. This animal has powerful claws for breaking open the nests of honeybees to get at the larvae and honey.

Out in the meadow, honeybees may fall prey to spiders; they can be trapped in orb-webs spun between flowers. But many are victims of a very sneaky attack by crab spiders. These spiders do not spin webs. Instead, they lurk underneath a flower and wait for a visiting insect. While the insect – which is often a honeybee – feeds, the crab spider crawls up from under the flower and pounces. With a sharp bite, the spider injects a poison which soon kills the bee; it then sucks up the body fluid of the bee.

In Africa and India, the Honey Badger, or Ratel, preys on both hives and wild nests. It uses its powerful front claws to break into a colony and steal pieces of honeycomb. The Honey Badger is often led to a colony by a most unusual accomplice, a bird called the Honeyguide. This bird feeds almost entirely on beeswax, but it is not strong enough to break into the nest. Instead, when it finds a honeybee's nest, it looks for a Honey Badger, or some baboons or even a person. Then, with a series of loud churring noises and a display of white tail feathers it attracts the attention of the animal or human and leads them to the nest.

The Honeyguide perches quietly in a nearby tree while the animal breaks open the nest to get at the honey. It waits patiently until the animal has finished feeding. Then the bird swoops down and feeds on the pieces of broken honeycomb.

A victim of a sneak attack, this honeybee is being eaten by a crab spider on the flower of a Dog Rose.

The Meadow Grasshopper shares its home with visiting honeybees.

Friends and neighbours in the meadow

For honeybees, the meadow is a place to visit for food. Here, they may come into contact with many other kinds of animals for whom the meadow is their permanent home. Some, like butterflies and hoverflies, share the honeybee's interest in flowers as refuelling stations. But, unlike the honeybee, these insects may also have other reasons for visiting flowers; for many insects, flowers are also a meeting place where males and females can find each other in order to mate and for robberflies, which prey on other insects, the flowers make excellent lookout platforms from which to pounce on unsuspecting victims. Sometimes, the victim is a honeybee.

The meadow is also a home for grasshoppers and bushcrickets. Very often, these insects can only be heard rather than seen. On hot afternoons, they chirrup and sing to each other; their colours so match their background that they are well-protected from the attentions of birds like the kestrel. This lovely bird hovers over the meadow, using its keen eyesight to detect small animals such as mice and beetles. But they protect themselves by using the dense jungle of stalks and stems as a hiding place, venturing out mainly under the cover of darkness. Other creatures which live in this way include millipedes, centipedes and snails. So the honeybee workers, plying their busy trade across the meadow, are the unsuspecting neighbours of many 'mini-beasts', all of which live and breed in the meadow.

This edible snail is one of the 'mini-beasts' of the meadow.

A satisfied bumblebee flies away from a Delphinium.

The honeybees' neighbours include other kinds of bee, many of which compete with the honeybees for the food provided by the meadow's flowers. The presence of the fat, furry bumblebees in the meadow may, however, benefit the honeybees in an interesting way. There are two kinds of bumblebee: those species which have long tongues and which can probe deep into tube-shaped flowers for nectar; and other species which have short tongues and which cannot normally reach the nectar in deep flowers. The short-tongued bumbles often steal nectar from deep-tubed flowers, such as Comfrey, by using their strong jaws to bite a hole near the base of the tube. In this way, they get at nectar normally reserved for bumblebees with longer tongues.

Then, along come the honeybees, always ready to take advantage of any opportunities. They use the holes made by the bumblebees to rob the Comfrey flowers of nectar. The jaws of worker honeybees are not strong enough to bite the holes, so they rely on the bumblebees to do it for them. By using these holes, the honeybees touch neither the male nor the female parts of the flowers; thus by robbing nectar they do not help in the pollination of the Comfrey flowers.

A honeybee pillages a Comfrey flower.

Bees help to pollinate the fruit trees when their hives are placed temporarily in this orchard.

Honeybees and people

Honeybees have always been valuable to people as a source of honey and wax. Honey was once the only sweetener available. Even today, for people in Africa, honeycombs and bee grubs are a valuable food, especially as a standby in times of shortage.

True beekeeping began when people moved wild colonies of bees in, perhaps, hollow logs, closer to their settlements so that they could protect them. Many peoples, in several parts of the world still do this today. Although we now keep bees in modern hives, we have not really domesticated the honeybee in the same way as we have domesticated the cow and the dog; we have hardly changed the behaviour of bees and even a modern beekeeper is still really just a honey robber.

Honey remains a valuable food source today, and the annual world honey crop is worth hundreds of millions of pounds. Countries like Canada, Mexico and Australia are the main exporters of honey.

The crops pollinated by honeybees are even more valuable than the honey that the bees produce. Many fruit farmers pay beekeepers to place hives in their orchards during the springtime blossoming of apple, pear and almond trees. And in North America, many beekeepers live a migratory life: they start their year in the southern states, where spring is early and the fruit trees flower first. Then, as the spring weather and flowering season move north, the beekeepers follow, transporting their hives on special trucks from farm to farm. The farmers benefit by having their fruit crops pollinated and the beekeepers enjoy a high yield of honey from the fruit blossom.

The wax from the honeycomb is also valuable. It is used in cosmetics such as lipstick and to make fragrant candles. Even the poison produced by workers is useful and drugs are made from it.

Because honeybees have been so important to people for so long, it is not surprising that there are many legends and beliefs about them. People used to think that the queen was male and in fact called her the 'king'. They believed that the king bee ruled over a kingdom of obedient subjects – the workers – and thought that the honeybee colony was a good example to people of how they should live.

As recently as the beginning of this century, beekeepers all over Europe felt they could be sure of their bees' loyalty and hard work if the bees were included in family celebrations. If there was to be a wedding, the beekeeper would decorate his hives with lace and ribbons and provide the bees with pieces of wedding cake. Similarly, if there was a death in the family, the hives would be decked out with black cloth as a sign of mourning.

If the beekeeper died, a close relative or his widow would go around the hives and tell the bees the sad news. This was supposed to make the bees accept a new master and work for him just as hard as they had done for the old beekeeper. 'Telling the bees' of a death was common all over Europe and the custom was brought to North America by the earliest settlers.

> Left, *a bronze bee decorates the lid of a perfume oil burner which dates from the Gallo Roman period, 300 AD.* Right, *an illustration from a 15th century Italian herbal from the Library of the Este family.*

Life in the meadow

The plants and animals in a rich meadow depend on each other for survival. Many animals eat the plants; others feed on smaller animals which have in turn eaten plants. For the honeybee and the myriads of other insects which live in or visit the meadow, it is the flowers which provide food and act as vital refuelling stations. These insects, including honeybees, are in turn eaten by a variety of animals. So, food and energy pass from the plants to the animals through what we call a 'food chain'. We can show how the honeybee is part of a food chain by a diagram in which the plants and animals are linked together because of what they eat.

All bees, including honeybees, have a very important position in the food chain. By pollinating flowers, they encourage the production of seeds and ensure future generations of flowers on which they and other insects can feed.

Food chain

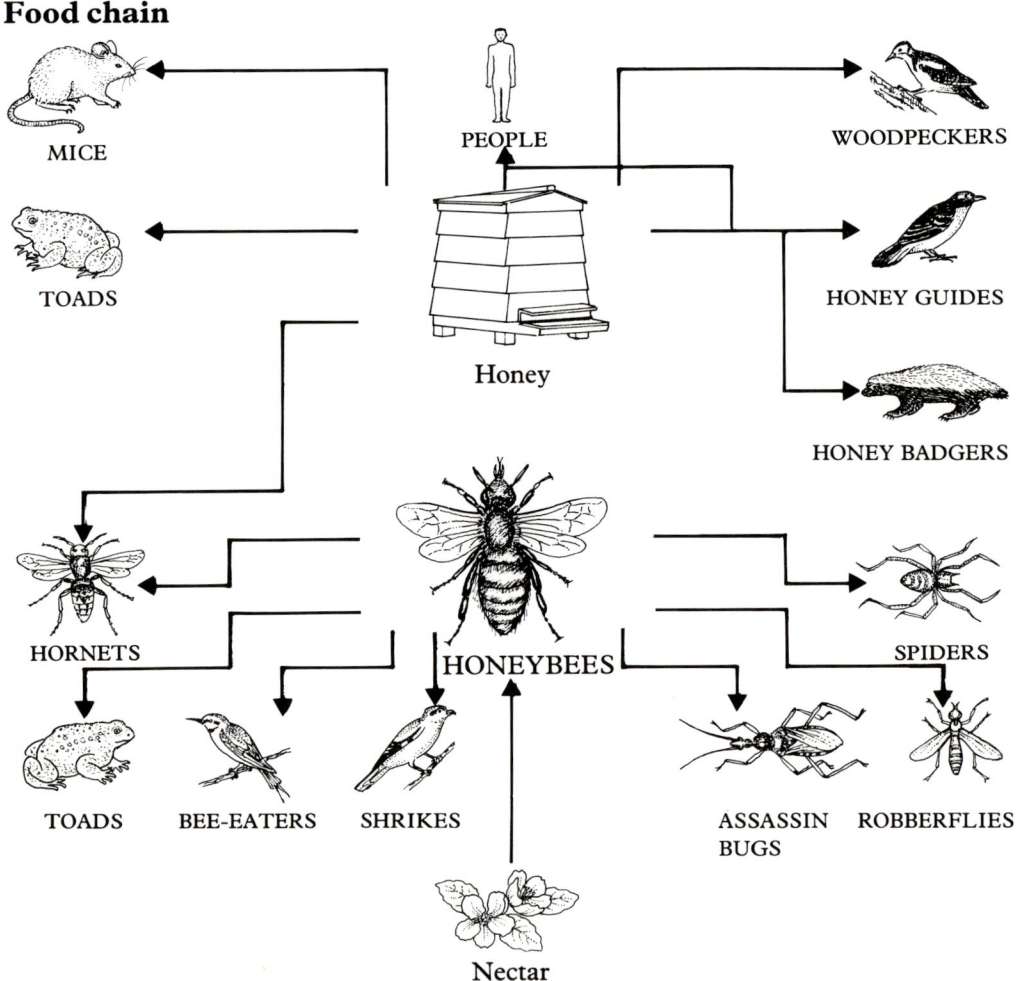

A honeybee worker packs pollen into the pollen baskets on her hind legs as she leaves a pear blossom.

Grazing animals are important, too. They keep down the coarse grasses and allow a profusion of wild flowers to grow. When rabbits were nearly wiped out in Britain because of the disease myxamatosis, the number of species of wild flowers decreased in many areas and with their decline, there were fewer wild bees.

The boundary hedge surrounding the meadow is an important part of the meadow habitat. It has its own species of flowers and acts as a natural 'corridor', for bees and other insects travelling through the countryside. Trees in the hedge and the field act as landmarks for honeybee workers returning to the hive. Hollow trees may even provide a place for honeybees to nest.

Unfortunately, these flower-rich meadows are becoming rare in our countryside. This is because much farming land is now cultivated for crops, while fertilizers and other chemicals are spread onto the fields to kill 'weed' flowers and encourage the grass or the crop to grow.

Many people, including wildlife and conservation groups, are trying to encourage farmers, land-owners and town planners to create meadow *habitats* both in the countryside and in towns. Some town and city parks now have special wildlife areas where meadow plants can grow. And many roadside verges, if mowed and managed properly, can be ablaze with wild flowers in spring and summer. You can even create a mini-meadow in your back garden – it is bound to attract honeybees, as well as butterflies and lots of other wildlife – to make it a special wild place of your own.

Glossary

abdomen: the rear of the three body parts of an insect 6, 8, 9, 19

antennae: feelers on the head which are used for smelling and touching 7, 8, 11, 12, 16, 18

caste: one of several types of individual living in the colony of a social insect species 6

compound eye: an eye made up of thousands of facets, each with its own lens and nerve connection to the brain 7

drone a male honeybee, which develops from an unfertilized egg 6, 7, 8, 9, 10, 12, 13, 20, 21, 22

exoskeleton: the horny, outer shell of insects which encloses and protects the body and to which the muscles are attached 6

gland: a special part of the body where a chemical, often a scent, is made 9, 10, 12, 14, 17

habitat: the natural home of an animal or plant 31

honeycomb: the double-sided array of thousands of six-sided, wax cells in which honeybees store honey, and rear brood 3, 8, 15, 18, 25, 28, 29

larva/larvae: the form of an insect which emerges from the egg 10, 11, 13, 14, 15, 20, 24, 25

nectar: a sweet sugary liquid produced by plants and made into honey by bees 3, 4, 7, 15, 16, 18, 23, 27

ocellus/ocelli: simple eyes, found in insects, with a single thick lens which can sense changes in the brightness of daylight 7

pheromone: a chemical messenger or scent produced by one animal which affects the behaviour of another individual of the same species 7, 12, 17

proboscis: tubular structure like a drinking straw through which insects suck up liquid food 7

pupa: the stage in the growth of an insect when much of the larva is broken down and re-formed into an adult 10, 11, 13, 24

queen: the egg-laying female caste in social insects 6, 7, 8, 9, 10, 12, 13, 15, 20, 21, 22, 23

queen substance: a pheromone produced by glands in the head of a queen honeybee, which prevents workers from rearing other queens and laying eggs 12, 23

royal jelly: a special food made in the heads of worker honeybees, which is fed to larvae 10, 13, 14, 20

spermatheca: a small bag or compartment of a female insect, in which sperm from males is stored after mating 20, 22

thorax: the middle of the three body parts of an insect, containing the flight muscles and bearing the wings and six legs 5, 8

The line drawings are by Lorna Turpin

First published in Great Britain 1990
by Belitha Press Ltd
31 Newington Green, London N16 9PU
Text © Oxford Scientific Films 1990
Consultant Editor: Jennifer Coldrey
Art Director: Treld Bicknell   Design: Naomi Games
ISBN 0 947553 57 6
Printed in the United States
No part of this publication may be reproduced; stored in a retrieval system, or transmitted, in any form or by any means, electronic, mechanical, photocopying, recording or otherwise, without the prior permission of the publishers.
British Library Cataloguing in Publication Data for this book is available from the British Library.

The author and publishers wish to thank the following for permission to reproduce copyright material: **Oxford Scientific Films Ltd.** for pp 6 *both*, 7, 8, 10 *both*, 11 *both*, 12, 13, 14, 15 *both* 16, 17 *below*, 18, 20 and 22 *above* (David Thompson); title page, pp 3, 4 *below*, 5 *above*, 28, 31 and back cover (G. A. Maclean); pp 17 *above*, 22 *below*, 23 and 27 *below* (G. I. Bernard); pp 4 *above* and 26 *above* (Mike Birkhead); front cover (Sean Morris); p 2 (Stan Osolinski); p 5 *below* (Alastair Shay); p 9 *left* (J. A. L. Cooke); p 21 (Georgina Dew); p 24 (Michael Fogden); p 25 *below* (Derek Bromhall); p 26 *below* (Martin F. Chillmaid); p 27 *above* (John Cheverton); Carolina Biological Supply Co. for p 9 *right;* Partridge Productions Ltd. for p 25 *above* (Anthony Bannister); and p 19 Photographie Giraudon, Paris for p 29 *both*.